Creatively Successful®

Strategies on "How To" Gain and Leverage Authentic Longevity in Success

By Tiana Allen
Healer, Teacher and Entrepreneur

Table of Content

Introduction 5

Chapter 1 Cutting ties with expectations 9

- A letter to the door
- Prosperity next exit

Chapter 2 Success = Sacrifice 13

Chapter 3 Waiting for Validation 17

- Still Waiting?
- Honoring Your True Validation
- Emotion vs Intuition

Chapter 4 The Persecution Process 24

- Forgiveness vs Forgetting

Chapter 5 The Sellout 27

Chapter 6 Distractions 30

- Perfectionism
- The Wisdom Approach
- Haters
- Motivating Factors

Chapter 7 Becoming Creatively Successful 35

- Finding your talent
- Having an Aha Moment
- Volunteering

Chapter 8 – Are you Ready? 45

    The Social Scene

- Marketing
- Contracts

Chapter 9 – Authenticity in Leadership 54

Chapter 10 – Getting out of your own way 56

Chapter 11 – Standards of Business 58

- Setting Boundaries
- Business Standards & Self Care
- Self-Love
- Creating Longevity

Foreword

I stand out, and I know this. I could be in the middle of Times Square, fully covered and in nobody's way — and I will still be noticed. I stand out so much that it is difficult to discern whether people's looks, stares or words are negative or positive. I don't understand others' intentions, so I become defensive. This is why I prefer clear communication with the expression of feelings, and then actions that follow.

The realization that I stand out is alarming, and I don't like it. I actually don't want to. The attention from standing out disturbs and scares me because I can't seem to take the judgement that comes from this. I can't fathom why there are others who crave attention and notoriety and try so hard to be noticed. I may have been a civil rights or freedom fighter in my former life because standing up for what is right just comes natural to me.

I love myself and who I am, but sometimes, I just want to be left alone. But, God has called me to be a representative of the light because he needs me for others. Now, I have to deal with standing out. For God, I will; however, I can't seem to break my defenses from the judgment. I'm always seemingly fighting for something. I ask God for permission to give up because I just want the negative feelings and emotions that come from fighting for what's right to go away. But God always reminds me to keep going.

I am an extrovert, but I get physically tired from the stress of standing out so much. I try to revert back, but I still get found. Always. So I stay quiet.

I still get judged anyway.

Speak or be silent; I still get found.

It is tiresome, and God is my only refuge. This is how He likes it. But, my spirit is drained because it is an ongoing battle. I want what God has for me, but I can't take the pressure.

And this is why I continue to go forward. This is how I know what I am doing is right. This thing called walking on purpose can drive anyone insane. I have heard the stories of many people who have given up due to others judgement, racism, ageism, pettiness and the sheer pressure of success. This will not be me. I only gain. This is why I go forward. God has my back, and he restores my energy when it is drained. Worship and love through meditation, prayer and writing sustains me. Because I don't want to do it, am tired, and mentally drained, I know I am ready. If I were not afraid it would be too easy, and I will surely fail on my own. I follow; therefore, I lead. No fear will win. The only blockage I have is internal. There is Only God! ~ Tiana Allen

Introduction

This book is to assist you in your journey.

You are definitely not alone. Believe me, I completely understand all the tiny little frustrating, yet freeing, particles that come along on the journey to success. God places us all on a journey that may be a bit difficult, but it is with those experiences that we have the honor of sharing with and assisting others on their path. Please know that.

It is through all my experiences that I've come to write this book.

If you are questioning choices you made in your career or education, you may find solace if you keep reading. This might be the much-needed tool to assist you in finding and utilizing your full creative potential that can be used to your advantage.

This book is comprised of several of my personal success secrets: learning to listen to God's voice, finding my calling, taking steps out on faith, and following through with things I wasn't aware I knew how to do!

> *"I choose to affect change, I choose to speak up. For all the other dominos to fall one has to fall first which leaves the other choice less to do the same. Being a domino means speaking up and doing the things that are difficult especially when they're needed.... A lot of times people think that we are fearless we are not fearless were not unafraid of the consequences of the sacrifices we have to make by speaking truth to power, what happens is we feel like we have to because there are too few people in the world willing to be the domino and take that fall. We are not doing that without fear."*
>
> *~Luvvie Ajayi, Author, Speaker, Professional Troublemaker*

Breaking Generational Curses. (extended intro)

Wisdom is what they say I have. Both my parents called it mother-wit. The youngest child is almost always the observer. I guess I was a sponge for watching others and learning what not to do because I've seemingly lived my life quite opposite than my siblings; although not moving too far away to be succumb to the generational curses that has plagued our family line. We are a lot like our parents and they are like theirs. However where one of my siblings sat down and stopped, I refused to give up. For that, I have conquered a few of the obstacles even my grandparents faced.

I was the first grandchild to get a full college degree and a masters. I am fulfilling my father's legacy of running a successful business, and am speaking around the country and abroad as he always wanted to. I am a teacher like my maternal grandmother; and a healer like my paternal grandma. I have a powerful - magnetic energy and love of people like my mother and am mysteriously strong like both my grandfathers. But, unlike them I have learned to channel these ancestral similarities and the things they might have seen as weaknesses into my strengths. I know that I have conquered their fears for them and have broken many generational curses by doing this.

Honestly speaking I am everything a lot of people in my family in the past were afraid of becoming. Successful. People have told me that I am very intimidating and have a powerful presence when I walk into the room. But I don't know anything about that I just know I walk with the light. And if following God, loving what I do and being creatively successful is provoking others to see their potential in breaking cycles of generational curses, I'll take that. So reader, before you start talking about generational wealth have a conversation with the elders in your family to determine what generational curses you need to break. Believe me it will open you up to a world of options when deciding your next steps on this journey.

When I tell people that I love my career, many ask me how I came to that point. I always respond the same. It takes a lot of **prayer**, a great deal of **persistence**, followed by unwavering faith & **passion.** Most importantly, I tell them that my career enhances who I am and allows me to understand and use my creative potential. Now I'd like to share this with you. Here are 11 of my trade secrets on how to I found my creative voice. I hope to help you find yours.

Chapter 1:
EXPECT OF YOURSELF A LITTLE MORE THAN AVERAGE. GOD IS RIGHT ABOVE THAT!

How many times have you gotten all excited and riled up about a certain person or opportunity that "magically" came your way? Have you ever taken a giant leap of faith only to get gravely disappointed in the end? You may talk to your friends and family, just to find out no one has a valuable, nor valid, explanation for what you are going through. It's because they, themselves, may not even know what to do if they were in that situation. Overall, you feel alone and counted out, with no one to consider your feelings, nor make you feel better. You are stuck with your thoughts, which sometimes escalate to frustration and lead to unfavorable reactions.

Closed doors are more of a blessing than open ones. Sometimes, God would let you walk through the very door you cried for him to open, just to teach you that he is in control of what you need on your journey. With this said, how many times do we still try to go back through those closed doors when we felt desperate, lonely and in need?

It's time to lower the expectations of other people and things and give yourself permission to expect more of yourself.

Knowing the right time to leave your comfort zone in order to move to the next level is critical. In most cases, it will be completely plain and clear to you. We all have had our fair share of challenges. Not that we have to redeem ourselves or prove anything to anyone — but truth is, being a leader is hard. Moving to the "next level" will present to you challenges beyond what you think you can stand. Do you really want to be *successful*? Well, be prepared to lose the things you thought you needed and gain the things you thought you didn't.

Please note, again, this will be very hard to do but here's a suggestion. Write a letter to all your disappointments, loses, expectations and those who provoked them. Reference all the things you've lost then list all you've gained. Acknowledge how you feel; acknowledge who is responsible for these feelings. Lastly, weigh the difference of the two categories and decide how you will/have moved on from it.

A letter to the door: Cutting ties with expectation

Dear door, you were never for me. You are an illusion of the truth. You wasted my time and energy trying to fool me into prying you open, but you rejected me and turned to stone. I was a fool for tying my emotions to you, but now, I see your true intentions. I am so glad you never opened for me because you would have sent me down the wrong road. You can remain closed for me. I am okay with this. I have found keys to others. I've also found patience. The doors that are for me will be opened, but you will still be under the same curse. Remaining where you are: closed and unchanged. I am so grateful to have freedom from the fear of rejection. Now, I can walk through any door as my authentic self. Thank you for not accommodating me.

Sincerely,

A Creatively Successful Alchemist

Prosperity; Next Exit

Never be afraid of being different. Always surprise yourself.

Everyone struggles; it's how we persevere through it that makes us stronger. There are so many options in this world, and it is easy to make any decision. The hard part is deciding which decision is best for you. This is why laying the groundwork to source your creativity is fundamental before considering beginning any business venture.

Creativity is a gift. Open it. First question:

Q: What is the one (1) career you always saw yourself in but never went after?

Give yourself a moment to think about it. I know there might be many ideas floating through your head, but let's try to hone into just one for now. If you are anything like me, you are a cross between a visual and kinesthetic learner. This means that if you don't actually explain your thoughts clearly and do something tangible when they emerge, they will leave your head just as quickly as they came. Even if you tried to remember them later on, they just won't seem to come back how you visualized them before. Am I right?!

This happens to me a lot! My ideas always come to me when I am nowhere in the vicinity of a pen/paper, actually they tend to come more when I am driving or at work.

I'm saying this to let you know that no matter how lost an idea seems to get, no matter how much you get distracted, and no matter how much you distance yourself away from a thing — if it is chosen for you, guaranteed it will always come back! God does things full circle. The instant he gives you a vision is the moment it all begins.

We all hear that call toward doing a certain thing but being open to it is a whole different ball game. We will discuss this more in future chapters.

As humans, we unfortunately tend to do what is more comfortable for us rather than what is best. That's because often times, what is best for us is not comfortable for us to do. Moving in the direction of your calling can and will place you in some very unfamiliar situations. The moment you submit to this vision and say yes to the call is the very moment your whole scenery will look different. You will literally be entering a new universe. You will start to see other people's perspectives differently. Your work ethic will change. You may lose-and-gain-and-lose friends. Family will be different; everything will be different. You must be able to accept this on your path.

> *"Don't wait until everything is just right. It will never be perfect. There will always be challenges, obstacles and less than perfect conditions. So what. Get started now. With each step you take, you will grow stronger and stronger, more and more skilled, more and more self-confident and more and more successful."*
>
> *-Mark Victor Hansen*

Are you ready to write your letter to the door?

Chapter 2
Success=Sacrifice

It's funny when someone tells me that I make being a business owner look easy because I am always happy. They often ask me how to get into a similar field because they are unhappy with their current place of employment and want to make more money. It's definitely cool that I inspire and motivate others — but here is the thing: be inspired, be motivated, but never try to do as someone else does without realizing the hard work that they had to put into their achievements. Money does not buy true happiness and trying to copy someone else's vision will never blow over very well. If you don't understand what true sacrifice is, you'll give up as soon as you are hit with the first challenge.

Let's delve deeper into what "success" — in any form — looks like. How do you define being "successful?" Be careful with this answer because you just may get what you ask for.

Whatever your definition is, stay committed to it and understand that superficial success (money, material things) are temporary. If this is what you are asking for, please have a long-term game plan and the right team available to help you make the right decisions. Remember that starting a business, brand or idea will be very costly in the beginning.

There are no limits as to what you can do in life, career, etc., but with owning your own business, be prepared to absorb all of the risks! Almost everything will be your responsibility to sacrifice, handle, or prevent. This is why many people claim to be "ready," but once they see risks start to present themselves, they get scared, go into hiding, or stop.

Let's talk about some of these risks.

- **Loss of identity** – Listen up! When you tell God that he has full permission to reveal to you your gifts, he will do just that! Who you thought you were is gone, and who you never knew you were is revealed. You will be whisked away to a vortex where you will have tunnel vision of the heart. Some things you will love, some things you will hate — but you will never fully understand, nor have the ability to explain any of it!! Your identity will be washed away slowly, but surely, in what may seem like a grueling never ending saga, with many twists and turns, for many months/years before your true identity is revealed. Long story short, you will find out a lot more about yourself in business.
- **Surrender** - Mentally, spiritually, physically, personally… need I go on?? Like Abraham, Moses, Joshua, and Joseph in the bible, God had to take them from their norm and impart them in new territories to reveal their greatness. Even Jesus had to leave Nazareth to go to Jerusalem to perform miracles. Sometimes, in order to be *Creatively Successful*, you may have to respectfully leave who or what you thought you knew behind in order to embark upon a journey of your own, on your own.
- **FEAR** – One of the most common and most influential things that shape our decision making process is fear. This pesky distraction can make any person stop pushing forward toward a goal. Fear usually shows up in two forms:
    - Fear of success: The mere thought of the obligation that comes with being successful seems frightening to those who don't want to be in the spotlight. Think of your favorite celebrity or an infamous one for that matter. Celebs are consumed with attention all the time and can't seem to lead a normal life due to cameras and people always around them. There is

also fear of who to trust at this point. Trust is a tricky subject when it comes to entrepreneurship. This will be discussed a bit further in another chapter.
   - Fear of failure: Your mind asks, 'what if I don't succeed? What if I can't afford to do it? What does this person think of me? How does that person view my idea? How will I start? If I start, what will be the outcome? Where will I gain clients/customers? Who will buy my product? Is my service/product good enough? Am I good enough? Sometimes the questions go downhill from there and lead to depression and giving up on your dream all together. Guess what, we all have those questions! The trick is sometimes you just have to put fear in a serious chokehold. Use self-love and tell yourself how great you are. Know your self-worth but never forget two things: 1) who you are serving (who your customer/client base is) and 2) why you are doing what you are doing! Fear runs away from this. Always. Combating fear means finding confidence. Fear is an illusion. It captivates and holds you hostage from achieving your goals and hog-ties you to its lies. Break free of this with confidence.
- **The beating, the shaking, and the pressing** – We are unique in our kind. No one will ever understand the life of an entrepreneur unless they have the calling to be one. This we must understand; clearly.
- **Constant loss** – Most of us would not like to hear this; but truth is, you will lose quite a few things. Some things you lose may superficially bruise your skin, while others will hurt deeply to the bone. You lose things when you sacrifice. Period. But what you will gain will be worth more than anything that can never be taken away. Happiness.

- **Constant gain** – Speaking of losses, sometimes in the binge of success you may reap access gain. Now this sounds glorious doesn't it? We do start businesses and seek life advice to have gain, right? Well sometimes in the wake of us having "everything we ever wanted" It can cause a divide within. Sure you will have more onlookers and friends, more money, etc... but what profits a man to gain the world and loose his soul? (Matthew 16:26) There is no point in having gains in success if you have lost yourself. We must seek who we are first on this journey; anything you place before this is a distraction and will for sure throw you off course.

The reality is, you can't be "successful" if you haven't failed at anything. For if we never fail, we'd miss out on an opportunity to learn ourselves. Pursuing a passion is hands down one of the toughest things anyone can do! It's bad enough that we have to struggle to figure it out first, but actually taking that first step to go for it takes a lot! And not only does it take a lot out of you, it takes a lot from you! All the sacrifices and hard decisions you'd have to make; leaving people behind, bringing new people in, settling in a new place, trusting your gut and God at the same time — it is a whirlwind of mixed emotions, doubt, assurance, fire and passion all thrown together in a gigantic ball of dynamite that could explode at any given moment. Whoever said pursuing your passion was easy has obviously gotten it completely twisted!

Now, don't get me wrong. It is a gift to be in tuned enough with yourself and God to know that you've been called out on a mission that is your vision and passion, but it is much easier said than done. The most beautiful thing about it is if we stop worrying about what isn't changing and focus on what already has we'd understand that God will always keep his word and provide. Success = Sacrifice; just like the earth, we all have seasons. Make sure you are properly prepared for the element of change.

Chapter 3
Waiting for validation:

To validate is to prove that something is acceptable. As entrepreneurs, we know we are limitless; however, it gets so cloudy when we have so many options to choose from and are the only ones to supply the answer. The feeling of being unsupported on your journey is quite real.

Needing validation really means you are seeking some type of support or looking to someone else for answers that you have the responsibility to know. Honestly, finding someone who "gets it" is rare because loyalty is fleeting. It is a long walk to purpose, and it is possibly one of the loneliest journey's anyone can ever be on.

Everything you need is hidden in self-love. It is pertinent that you know this!! If we stop seeking your worth through other people and material things we'd find that self-doubt is a ruthless enemy to our spirit that you must not give any power to! Marianne Williamson said it best "Our deepest fear is that we are inadequate..." Why do we tend to focus on what we "cannot" do, rather than what we "can?" Did you know that with your gifts you have the power to control your own destiny and create your own success stories?! Let's get real with ourselves. You are powerful beyond measure, Dig deep within and be content with your true authentic self. We will speak more on Self Love in Chapter 11.

It's a shame that in today's society we are boxed into categories based off race, age, gender, made up generations, etc... and are given false validation by being told how we are supposed to behave based off of these categories. The reality is that no one fits any particular mold, rather we aren't supposed to. If this is one of your hindrances, here is a little motivation for you.

We were created to create! We design memories out of momentum, manifest reality out of dreams, our future from our past, and most importantly, we create life out of something that wasn't!! But, a large percentage of incomplete missions are due to us succumbing to other people's opinions and or lack of support — which, ironically enough, are two things we seek out the most on our journeys. Listen, don't ever allow someone to tell you that you aren't creative enough to do a certain thing. Your gifts were not given to them, they were directly given and tailor made just for you.

Being led or called out to do a certain thing is fulfilling; yet, there are tons of emotions attached. We are well aware of our goals, tasks and assignments. We are dead-set on our mission. All of our senses are perfectly open to know what's next for us to do. However, we are numbskulls when it comes to our surroundings. Even if we can sense that a situation isn't right, we tend to proverbially sweep it under the rug or pick the absolute wrong time to handle it. This is because our focus, although it is on point for our purpose, is tunnel vision. This is why we are so shocked when someone competes with us, or when a situation pops out the blue. We are often left with the question, "What did I do to deserve this??" When this happens — which will be often — this means you are not following our intuition.

When you are standing on the edge, it's hard to discern whether something is what you think you want to do versus what your gut says. We rely on our reactions to things to bring us validation but don't lie to yourself and call it intuition. That's contrary to the point. If you know something isn't right to do or say, but you do it anyway, you are the only person to blame. Period.

As humans, we get so tied up in how we feel in the moment and mix up God's voice with our own. This hinders us from doing what we felt was right in the first place. My friends, to truly be *Creatively Successful*, you must not be afraid to fly or fall flat on your face because unbeknownst to you, if we are not listening properly, that fall will not be pretty; it will hurt, but if you are in tuned enough you'd be alright.

Listen, taking the initiative to step into leadership as an entrepreneur, shifting gears in life, or to step out of the corporate arena isn't an easy task, it's daunting, uncertain and scary. No one who truly loves what they do stays all in because it's fun or for the crackerjack prize at the end. If you are reading this book you have chosen to consider taking one of the previous steps. We seek validation from various sources but gain clarity on the fact that you are lead in such a way that no one would understand unless they were in it themselves. Yes, we love what we do, but that is only because we remember what we've been through to get where we are. Furthermore, we remember who or what carried us through.

Still waiting to be validated?

You claim you want it, but let's be honest. Are you prepared to do the work that is required of you to become successful, or are you idly asking and waiting for deferred dreams to magically come true? Finances got you at a stand-still? Are you trying to finish or complete something first, waiting on a friend or family member to validate you through a compliment, waiting for someone to "give you a chance" or are you one of those still waiting on the right "time?" It's time to step into reality. Success is not given; it is made through conscious thinking and proactive doing.

Unfortunately though, many people live their whole lives completely missing out on how great they are because they are waiting and or wanting someone else to show them where the easy button is. And in this process, they tend to forget that they are the ones fit to handle the tasks of success, even with their flaws, limitations and all!

Your creative edge is what has been instilled and engrained in you, so you can never lose what you already have. Successful people think differently. We waste tons of energy trying to prove ourselves — when in reality, we were never meant to be understood. Stop trying to "explain" your vision, ideas and mission to those who can't comprehend. My advice to you is "Leave them where they are and keep it moving." We never cease to learn, therefore we never cease to teach. In the end trust your faith and know that you are not alone! We are all, in some way, on the journey to be creatively successful.

Following your intuition (your true validation)

Intuition is very important in both personal relationships as well as in business. This is your red flag, your target, your bullseye and the number one answer to your questions. Understand where your motivation truly begins. You can hear wise words from other sources, go to inspirational seminars, and follow your favorite subject matter gurus; however, if your hands and feet are not moving to do your own work, then you'll never find success — nor will you hear your own voice.

Intuition can easily be mistaken for Emotion. How many times have we ran off of adrenalin whenever we got too happy or too frustrated and reacted without thinking? I know I can count several! Well this is indicative of allowing your emotional self to drive you. Your intuition can be still or loud. It's a feeling in the pit of your stomach, a racing heartbeat, a force that can either knock the wind out of you or make you swallow it. It can be an inner shout that comes from your conscious as if your brain was trying to talk to you. On a metaphysical level some people see signs within the earth, have vivid dreams, journal or even have the ability to just "know" when something is or isn't good for them.

Being intuitive is a trait we all have but some of us are too afraid to tap into it. Being able to recognize the difference between emotion and intuition can be tough and does take time. As we discuss further on intuition vs emotion observe the chart on the next page. Look at the characteristics of emotion. Ask yourself which do I feel more of what do I need to work on? Then take a look at Intuition. How does this characteristic align with your emotions? In order to end the unnecessary wait for someone else's approval / validation and open up to your creativity in business and life; this chart may help you better understand our emotional and intuitional capabilities.

Emotion vs Intuition

Emotion	Intuition
Happiness	Listening to and understanding the source of your Emotion
Crying	
Frustration	
Joy	
Anger	
Irritable	
Sternness/ Mean	
Reverted	
Energetic	
Fear	
Argumentative	
Excessively Nice/ Giving	
Defensive	
Controlling	
Scared	
Silent	
Talkative	
Overthinking	
Reactive	
Passionate	
Depression	
Courage	
Hate	
Observant	
Love	
Panic/Anxiety	

It's hard to decipher your emotional self from your intuition. Sometimes they both feel the same. Empath's (which is what I am) tend to feel everything. We come across very passionate because our empathy overshadows logic to a point where we are completely led by emotion. Sometimes it gets the best of us because we are reactionary and don't listen first. Empath's have to be very careful to understand our strengths and weaknesses in order to draw boundaries over our threshold. Read more on Empaths at www.WriteAsPrescribed.com. If we are more technical / analytical we thrive off of gaining as much knowledge about a thing to the point where we get isolated, shut in and introvert ourselves. We have so much information about a lot of things but not enough social skills to be able to apply it. For those of us who are "helpers" we tend to attract those who are in a constant state of "need." We tend to place our own needs aside and draw nearer to them because we feel like it is a part of our duties to scoot everyone on their way. When we do this we lower our "see levels" You see, we easily define ourselves by our emotions and are blinded by how making an emotional decision can in our way.

Overall reflecting back to the chart in the beginning having emotion isn't a bad thing. It is a part of what makes us human. Being intuitive is a trait we all have that opens up to us once we observe our actions and listen to ourselves. It's not about being overly emotional or not emotional enough, It's about our reactions and responses to them. Validation is no longer needed after this is understood. In chapter 11 I discuss a powerful way to break free from emotional ties and provide tips that may be of benefit to you on your journey.

Chapter 4

The persecution process

Long story short, you ask the right questions, you get the right answers. You also get what you prepare for. Are you prepared for the answers?

Your past can be one of your greatest teachers. The Bible states, "Love those who persecute you" but sometimes the cut is so deep that you just want to feed them back the same energy. I get it. Playing fair when you are hurt can be extremely hard because you are reacting out of emotion (remember Chapter 3's conversation?) That "be positive turn the other cheek" thing gets conflicting when you are on track and seemingly doing everything right, but someone or something comes along to try to remind you of things you may have done wrong. Hang-ups that you are still holding on to from your past can come to haunt you and make you miserable; but in the end, it is up to you how to rise above what happened, recognize your place in it, and seek self-healing. The only thing that other person should be held accountable for is doing the same; if they do not then it's their fate they are juggling with God; not yours.

Circumstances come to persecute you through happenstance, financial challenges or people you trust and love the most. These situations make a mockery of your calling. They come from out of nowhere, just when you think you are content or are on the brink of God doing something greater in your life. It's almost as if they say, how dare you have a vision? How dare you dream big and trust God? How dare you feel like you deserve better? Don't you know that you are supposed to remain where you are forever? You can't grow. I won't let you!! In one of my favorite books, *The Dream*

Giver, by Bruce Wilkinson, Wilkinson calls this phenomena as "Border Bullies;" basically stating that in the end, you shouldn't fear circumstance, circumstance should fear your imagination! Your creativity should rule the moment; circumstance has no control! You do! You are a beast! A creative intellect with a brilliant mind. If you know who you are, then you know exactly where you are going. No one can change that. As for me...

I laugh in the rain. HECK, I'd even take a jog in heels.

When you make a decision to embark on to a new thing in life, persecution seems inevitable. Sometimes when it rains, it pours — and sh** happens in storms! But, there is great news about this. That inspirational quote about, "not having sunshine without the rain," is true! Fun fact: Scientists state that rain is actually fresh water. And get this, it literally clears the air!! Sounds like something we really need right?

Needless to say, when you are having a hard time, broken focus, life issues, financial worries, fear, etc., you are not alone! I will reiterate that statement many times more in this book, just to show how important it is. We are not alone in our issues. Just like you are going through it, someone else has actually, already been where we are before. Actually, there is a possibility that over a third of the people we encounter on a daily basis may have experienced a similar thing.

Forgiveness vs Forgetting:

No matter what that nursery rhyme says — in reality, words can really hurt!!! However, you should never allow then to interfere with your blessings! Maybe that person had noticed something in you that they are seeking. Overall sometimes we take things personally. The "attack" may be directed at you but in actuality their negativity steamed from a deeper part of themselves that they were misdirecting at you. When this happens in order for you to keep your energy centered and balanced the best response is to say nothing and choose to be happy, not irritated or frustrated. This could lead to bitterness and a block on your growth and blessings. Trust me, I've been irritated many times in my journey and annoyed with other people, things, circumstances, and even myself. One thing I know for sure is this has never stopped me from pursuing my end result or remembering my why. I always stick to my bottom line, no matter what. That keeps me grounded and motivated. Maturity is key and there's nothing wrong with speaking up for yourself and protecting your mission. Sometimes that other person needs to be told this quote by Joel Osteen: "If you can't be positive, then at least be quiet."

To forgive or to forget — this is always a hot topic. To be honest many people are unsure which is which; thus they have a hard time figuring out what to do.

It's hard to gain your energy back after someone has hurt you and/or demeaned all of your efforts to help them along their paths. It hurts when people you've called friends and loved ones have turned on you and made you feel less than who you know you are. Like a movie with an interesting plot twist, it always catches you by surprise. Who do you turn to when the person you trusted is now your adversary? Do you let it go? Do you express your thoughts and feelings to them? Or, do you do both?

If letting go is the only option, then we all know it is easier said than done. How do you get over the shock? My advice is always remember your why. Understand your place in the issue. Return the other persons emotions back to sender and work on your own. Most issues are resolvable, and broken pieces can be glued back together depending on many there are to work with.

Sometimes, the only one stopping you is the person you see in the mirror. Never let anyone stop you from smiling but don't be afraid to speak your mind about how you feel. Some people just want to get a rise out of you or find something wrong in you to make themselves feel better. Furthermore, you don't have to explain your happiness to others that probe and prod you for, "what's underneath your smile." If you are truly happy in your gifts, your creative spirit won't even allow you to pay attention to negative things. Ideas will be flowing, you will be mad focused, and again — your work will speak for itself! The opinions of others shouldn't have ANY control over your greatness! Unfortunately, sometimes it does somehow gets in our vortex and as I stated before, words do hurt. But, how long you will allow the wound to stay open before you clean out the infection?

Finally, it's important to understand that all things begin and end with a decision. Persecution is an unfortunate part if the process when you yield to God. There are some people who can hear you speak a thousand words and still not understand you. And there are others who will understand without you even speaking a word. Basically, let your success be your noise. Say your peace by doing what brings you peace. Silence speaks louder than words, and some folks don't even deserve that! However, if you must speak how you feel, I am a huge advocate for transparency. Do not hold everything in. Say your peace quickly and move forward. There should be no reason to look back, other than to reflect on the lesson you've learned. Life happens to all of us its understanding what you are allowing it to manifest itself into that is your decision.

Chapter 5
The Sellout

Displaced, severely misjudged and under-characterized. This chapter is particularly short because I'd like to get straight to the point when I say this:

It's not uncommon for someone who is well aware of themselves to be targeted and cause confusion within the psyche of others. Quite frankly, we freak people out! This is true. Someone who is not self-aware tends to place blame on another person or other things to appease the lies they are telling themselves. This way it diverts the attention away from the confusion of how they are feeling. We *Creatively Successful* people tend to be their scapegoats (See Chapter 4 The Persecution Process). We are most likely to be labeled "sellouts" for not only thinking outside the box but for going for the better in our own lives.

Not everyone is rooting for you to succeed. We, unfortunately, are living in times where people would rather be "followers" than leaders. People would rather go for what's "trending" than utilize their own practical knowledge. Social media is a cultic world; but as a business owner, you have to be somewhat in it — otherwise, you'd be completely out of the loop.

With that said, people are more prone to "take" ideas from creative people rather than learn, face fears and grow on their own. For the people in your circle, sometimes it's like a tug of war between fitting in and standing out. You know very well you are working in your purpose and doing well for others and yourself, but the struggle is still very real! It's almost easier for everyone if you are not succeeding.

> *"We forget that our heroes are human. When you are looked at for your talent beyond your race, religion, etc. — that means you are beloved."* – Jill Scott

It's amazing how many opportunities have come to us that we missed out on. Our prayers are always heard and answered; it's our humanity that keeps us from discerning this. Why? Because we are looking for it to come how we want to see it. This is why people dare not to be creative. This is also why others label creatives as sellouts; it's quite ok to say that they really admire us.

There are too many people saying what they are, who they are, and what they can do, but when they are called upon these things and it's time to show and prove, all you can find of them is the box of excuses they've left behind. Some people want something they are not willing to do the work for! Period. Never be this type of person. Be the sellout. As a matter of fact, be a limited edition.

Chapter 6
Distractions, Haters and Motivating Factors

DISTRACTIONS are the root to all evil when it comes to getting tasks done. My biggest distraction, honestly, is myself. I have a tendency to want to get everything completed at once. When I set a goal, I am literally relentless in completing it (hence, how I finished a bachelor's degree and a master's in 3 ½ years. I wasn't playing anybody's games!) One other thing that distracts me are my thoughts. I have a very vivid imagination and a sharp memory; however, they tend to get jumbled together somehow into this alternate reality of some sorts. Needless to say, I daydream a lot. I am literally in my own head half of the day. I have to make myself write things down because seeing my own words on paper is the only thing that keeps me aligned. I look back at old journals and feel shocked at what I wrote. Sometimes, I think that my words aren't enough and feel the need to repeat and explain myself when speaking. But, the insight and clarity I have when I write gives me confirmation that I am wise beyond my own words, and that they are enough. If you are interested in Journaling please check out our Journaling Kits by visiting www.WriteAsPrescribed.com and follow us on social media @SelfLoveRX.

Distractions can be pitfalls in anyone's journey because they come to entice you to not complete a project. They come in various forms and test your patience only to redirect your priorities. How many times have you placed something on hold because a friend called, your favorite television show was on, you fell asleep or decided to step out to get some fresh air but when you got back to your project you've now completely lost your train of thought, better yet your interest in the entire thing? This happens a lot with entrepreneurs. This is because there was no clear plan of focus nor strategy to complete this particular project. We creatives tend to be kinesthetic and visual learners. We like to jump into an idea head on and understand all the details later.

So, how can we get out of our own way? Well, the circus that is constantly tumbling in our heads will make that hard to master but creating a focus plan can help. Write down your focus plan in the form of a priority list. Before you start mixing up your personal and business life make sure you are diligent in separating the two. It is important to understand that things have to be completed on both sides and contain the following things:

- First things first: Determine the first thing you need to complete. This could be something personal or business related whatever this thing is it needs to be done or in the process of.
- Make a distinction between what is personal vs business (this is very important because somehow these two cross paths and can seem interchangeable)
- Don't be afraid to have more than one set of priorities. We have multiple distractions and it is ok to have several priorities; just be sure to justify and label each in the order of its importance (this is important as well)
- List your distractions. The key is to be honest with yourself. Jot down if it is you that is causing or allowing these to happen or if it is circumstantial. Listing your distractions can determine what you see as controllable or beyond your control. Not only this but taking a look back at these notes in the future will show you what you were most concerned about and showcase the growth (or lack of) that had taken place from it.

- For every problem, there is a solution. So what are you going to do about it? Every action that takes place moving forward begins with a decision. Be sure to write make a POA (Plan of Action) and stick to it!
- Alright so we have our POA but there is another distraction possibly a stop out, financial issues, life happening, etc…write down your road blocks. Road blocks are tougher than distractions because they determine if you stay the course with the decision you have decided to make. Road blocks tend to get you in your feelings and have you replaying scenarios in your head as if you are making the wrong decisions. Depression, anxiety, and the dreaded FEAR begins to step in and creates this world of what if, maybe, and maybe not's. Being in your own head feels like you are in a movie where you are the only character (ever seen that film Castaway?) it's an ongoing saga that gets replayed relentlessly until you decide the ending.
- To combat being in your own head always remember your solution. Determine if these road blocks are giant boulders or tiny pebbles. Never forget the solution and circle back to your why (See Chapter 2 Success=Sacrifice). Even if you have to jot it down again there is always a space for this in your focus plan. If this gets too hard for you to draw up yourself, we have a solution for you! Download a copy of your focus plan by visiting www.WriteAsPrescribed.com.

Perfectionism

Being perfect is way too mundane and boring for a creative alchemist such as yourself. We actually hurt ourselves when we place too many high expectations on ourselves and of others (See Chapter 1, Cutting Ties with Expectations) Perfectionism is just misguided hyper judgement of yourself that can be directed toward "perfecting" every detail of your business, yourself and everyone else around you. Perfectionism is control. Understanding this is important because some of you may be dealing with this issue but are not aware. Listen, throwing all of your "control" in your business in the beginning just might be one of the smartest things anyone can do; it can also be one of the things that hinders you from your growth.

Learning from my beginnings in the early 2000's social media had not taken off like it currently is so I had to learn everything from scratch. With that, perfectionism set in like crazy. I knew everything, I had my set standards but it wasn't until I began to experience a bunch of failures and brick walls that I understood that I had no clue about boundaries. I was very open to supporting other people and because I thought I had everything under control with my brand I allowed them to enter into my professional space unprotected. This cost me a lot of time, energy and money that I could have spent learning myself more. My business wasn't perfect and I did not know everything. Just because I had learned the technical stuff from all of my educational excursions did not mean that I knew how to apply this knowledge. I was always 2-3 steps ahead of things but had to be thrown off my game to discern the difference between learned (technical/theoretical) information and wisdom.

The wisdom approach

Taking the high road is always hard especially if it seems like you have to level down from your creative free spirited self. I used to think that I had to solve and understand everything because it needed to be clear from my path. I did this until I realized that I was only allowing distractions to break me down which created an unawareness in my emotional space. As confident and self-aware as I was, I thought that protecting my knowledge and authenticity was more important and anyone/thing who challenged this needed to be handled. Not true at all. See, wisdom teaches us that these challenges are opportunities for growth and that is what needs to be recognized. Second protecting your emotional space is vital because that determines your reactions to these distractions and your POA for moving forward. It also helps you develop stronger boundaries. Wisdom is strategy.

Haters and Motivating Factors

Haters

Speaking of boundaries and wisdom lets briefly discuss a distraction that most of us may not even consider. Haters. Being a creative you will always gain a following. Some may just watch and mimic you while others will want to know more. But, hands down one of the most annoying distractions can be someone who just has a vengeance against you for whatever reason. Haters are bullies that can't discern between words, actions or silence. They already have their preconceived notions and feelings and are blinded by these.

Haters are blockers of your next level that come to shake up your faith and bring you back into their comfort zone. Most haters try to pull out insecurities in others so they could seem secure within themselves. Sometimes, we play it safe around haters just so we won't rile them up. But playing it safe appeases the hater. When you shrink it gives incentive for them to try to control you. A hater can't stand authenticity because they do not have any, nor are they secure with themselves. I'm pretty sure your hater doesn't even have a focus plan.

Meanwhile, we should be too busy creating to hate. You can be the best humanitarian, lover of all, positive-energy giver, animal lover, listener, doer for others, hopscotch and bubblegum person on the planet, but you will still encounter those energy vampires who thrive off putting their failures on you. Be open to learning but never forget what you are doing.

A wise person is always straight to the point. They know that calling a hater out for who they are is an option, but staying silent with no need to speak or be loud will do more damage. A silent person is always labeled as dumb or weak, but wisdom notifies them that by doing this, they have the power to provoke change. At first, they are mocked and misunderstood; but in the end, they are mimicked.

Never let the ignorance of others dictate your level of commitment to what's important. A hater is but a secret admirer in mediocre clothing. Never mind their insecurities. Be around those that will enhance your spiritual and intellectual growth and leave the others where they are.

Motivating factors

It all starts with a decision. The truth is you will always be your own worst enemy. What we allow will continue and the things we dismiss to look within ourselves will get projected onto someone else. Meanwhile God and the universe are waiting for you to acknowledge them to be your guiding force. No one else can dictate your next move but you. What you decide to focus on is 100% your own decision and cannot be blamed on anyone else. What decision are you prepared to make?

Chapter 7
Becoming *Creatively Successful*: What Good Is Talent If It Isn't Being Used?

If you haven't found your purpose yet, then keep looking — it may just be searching for you. Ask yourself this question, "What do I have in my hands?"

In Exodus 4, Moses asked, "What if they do not believe me or listen to me and say, 'The Lord did not appear to you?'"

The Lord said to him, "What is that in your hand?"

"A staff," he replied.

"Throw it on the ground," the Lord said. Moses threw it on the ground, and it became a snake, and he ran from it.

Moses then said, "Pardon your servant, Lord. I have never been eloquent, neither in the past nor since you have spoken to your servant. I am slow of speech and tongue."

The Lord said to him, "Who gave human beings their mouths? Who makes them deaf or mute? Who gives them sight or makes them blind? Is it not I, the Lord? Now go; I will help you speak and will teach you what to say."

But, Moses said, "Pardon your servant, Lord. Please send someone else."

Never allow what you think of as hindrances and insecurities stop you from staying faithful to your "why." It is dangerous to your spirit to have a gift and not know what it is nor its purpose or power. There are so many lost people in the world whom are unwilling to claim themselves. But; you were not made to be lost; here are some tips to help you find your talent.

According to the dictionary, the word talent is defined as *a special natural ability or aptitude; a capacity for achievement or success; ability; capability, gift, genius.*

The simple question is this: What good is talent if it isn't being used? Unfortunately there are many people who are unhappy with the decisions they've made in life, their careers, or their education. Many people crave happiness and financial stability but do not like the cards they have been dealt. This happens more often than not.

Maybe you are wondering how you can be content with or even love what you do. Or, maybe you are one that is trying to figure out how to following your passion. You have searched all over for that dream job, applied to dozens of places, and made more copies of your resume than you could stand; still, you have come out empty-handed. You were told you're not qualified enough or over qualified (side eye) — and you can't stand it! You are at your wits end with applications and have rummaged the earth looking for someone to give you a chance.

Well can you guess where the answer to this is? Have you looked at yourself lately? Yeah yeah I know this already you might say but; have you searched through your box of unused talent to see if you still have it? Think about these things: What are you good at, what areas have you grown, what are your weaknesses and how can you use this to your advantage?

Finding Your Talent(s)

1. **To find your talents you have to understand who you are.**
   Take learning and personality assessments. However hard pressed one may feel about these tests, there is always something to be learned by them.
   a. Take the Kolb Learning Style Inventory (LSI) Assessment to figure out your learning style. You will discover if you learn from experience (Diverging), reflecting (Assimilating), thinking (Converging) or doing (Accommodating).
   b. The Friends Learning Style Inventory will help you discover if you are an auditory, kinesthetic or visual learner.
   c. The Thomas-Kilmann Conflict Mode Instrument Assessment will allow you to discover how you respond to certain situations. You will learn if you are competing, collaborative, compromising, avoiding or accommodative in a situation.
   d. The Myers-Briggs Temperament Test will allow you to identify your personality. You will learn which one of the sixteen temperament types you are, and what they mean to you. It may also help find some of your talents.
   e. Also read author Steven Covey's *Seven Habits of Highly Effective People.* This book has greatly enlightened me. Covey states:

   "If you want to achieve your highest aspirations and overcome your greatest challenges, identify and apply the principle or natural law that governs the results you seek. How we apply a principle will vary greatly and will be determined by our unique strengths, talents, and creativity, but ultimately success in any endeavor is always derived from acting in harmony with the principles to which the success is tied."

2. **Channel your knowledge to find my talent.**

In *The Element: How Finding Your Passion Changes Everything*, Robinson & Aronica stated:

> *"We need to challenge what we take for granted about our abilities and the abilities of others. Part of the problem with identifying what we take for granted is that we don't know what they are because we take them for granted in the first place. They become basic assumptions that we don't question."*

This reminds me of the saying, "Everyone can teach you something, and no one is without some sort of knowledge in a certain area." My mission in this book is to assist you in channeling that knowledge and using it to your ability. Here are some talents, interests and hobbies you may have forgotten about. If any of these sound like they describe you feel free to jot it in your journal.

- I am a ***visual person***. I have a great eye. I am very observant and often see things others do not. I love looking at beautiful things like nature, the arts, pictures, etc.
- I work best when I am ***hands-on***; therefore I am kinesthetic. I like movement. I like to take things a part and fix them. I feel accomplished after I have seen something I have created.
- I am a ***great listener***. I could recall and repeat verbatim what I have heard and store it into my brain. Being auditory, people always come to me for advice. I also have a good ear for music.
- I am extremely ***creative***. I have the ability to transform almost anything into what I want it to be. I have a knack for getting around what seems like the toughest situations. When

I see an empty space or a place of chaos, I see opportunity to explore.
- I very ***analytical***. I like to think things through before I react. I am a deep thinker and could raise very intriguing questions in a conversation. I like to find solutions for answers. I like analogies, numbers and formulas.
- My voice is my greatest asset. I love to be heard and to speak my opinions. As a ***talkative*** individual, I love to network and meet new people. I love to share my experiences with others so they could learn from me.
- I love ***writing***. I have a creative imagination and like to make short stories from my daydreams. I enjoy researching and documenting theories and facts. I am very good with breaking down and understanding words.
- I am an ***athlete***. I enjoy sports, exercise, fitness and movement. I am ***competitive*** by nature. I love to teach people proper ways to take care of themselves.
- I am a ***compassionate*** person. I care about the wellbeing of others and am at my best when doing for them. I give my all to help those in need. I like to see people happy and fulfilled. If it were possible, I would give my services for free.
- I am a ***thrill seeker***. I live on the edge and always do things differently. I do not play by the rules and always find ways to make things enjoyable. I always have an interesting story to tell and am a joy to be around.
- I am great with fashion. People always ask about my ***sense of style***. I have a good eye for aesthetics. I could make what seems like the wrong combination seem right.
- I **manage *finances*** well.
- I consider myself a ***foodie***. I love to experiment and create dishes from scratch.

Have you had your Aha moment yet?

Having an Aha moment means that you have changed the way you perceive certain things in the world; or you've had a paradigm shift. Covey describes a paradigm as being *"like a pair of glasses affecting the way one sees things in life." (125)*

(Paradigm) Understanding first what you want in your vision, the socio-economic need for it, and how you are going to make it happen. (Paradigm Shift) As your vision pans out, and you see the results, you and everyone else understands why you worked so hard on it.

Think about your desires. Where do you see yourself in 5-10 years? Are you successful and happy, or are you still in the same spot? Think down the line to where you want to be and use this as a tool to be proactive with your talents.

Let's say you have a stable career; you are working very productively and diligently because you are content with having stable work; then, one day it hits you — you don't love what you do and this is not what you want to do with your life. There is another interest you want to pursue; however, your current career is providing you with the finances you need to support yourself. Out of fear, you push the other vision aside and pursue other ventures that take you off course. Your bright idea fades into a lingering thought, and your career becomes a job that you now dislike. The daily routine you were once productive in becomes painstakingly rough for you to complete. If this is you or sounds similar to you, then two things you crave are happiness and stability.

Complacency almost always leads to unhappiness, so think of ways to allow for growth. Ask yourself, how could I make my job into a career that I enjoy? Can my talents be utilized at the company in a way that would keep me employed, increase my skills and make me happy? Or, would I be able to grow better on my own?

Following a dream is difficult because it has the potential to be differed if not planned or though out properly. But, there is also fear of losing your job and financial resources. Fortunately, there are ways around this, which entail lots of sleepless nights and planning. If you want to keep your job, but your dream is calling you, then working on both could play in your favor. Work your job from 9-5 (or whatever schedule you have), and then develop your vision from 6-9 (or whatever time you go to bed). That way, you are both financially stable and developing your happiness.

Speaking of development, another great way to gain insight on a particular field of interest is to provide a service to a greater good.

Volunteering

A wise man once stated, "Success is not a destiny; it is a journey."

With this being said, if you still don't feel like you can figure out your plan of action then taking time out of your schedule to volunteer is always a good thing to do. It could also help move you in the direction you were meant to go. If you are trying to figure out what your passion or talent is, try volunteering at various places that fit your interest to get a feel for things. Let's say you have a desire to become a chef, but you don't know if you want to go to school, own a catering business or work for a restaurant there are dozens of organizations that could use the help of someone like you.

Volunteering is one of the most selfless acts any human can perform. You will definitely gain something from this. First and most importantly, you will get the opportunity to use your talents to help someone who is truly in need. Then, either one of two things will happen: 1) Your passion will thrive, and you will recognize the particular area you want to focus on; or 2) You will discover that what you thought you wanted to do is not for you, and move on to focus on something else. Whatever the take away is from volunteering, it will be a lesson learned on your journey.

Volunteering could also help you to gain referrals, contacts, and even a possible business relationship or associateship. Most importantly, it will either enhance your desires or help you move on to the next idea.

On a personal note volunteering has helped me truly tap into the avenue I really wanted to pursue in my company. I've volunteered in a variety of healthcare settings, hospitals, domestic violence shelters, literacy and educational institutions and even hospice facilities. All of these were great experiences that had a profound impact on me and sparked the beginning of me starting my own nonprofit organization *see: www.TheJourneyInstitute.org.*

Gaining ideas from volunteerism are good but there is even greater reward when you do it out of selflessness and gain a fullness within your spirit. With that one of the most fulfilling volunteer experiences I had come from doing missionary work in Haiti and Kenya. Working in third world countries with drastic impoverished communities really forces you to take a step back from yourself and focus on the direct need of the people you are serving. Being a missionary taught me invaluable lessons on how to discern true priorities and to embrace the simplicities of life. It also made me aware of the importance of knowing how you work individually so that your strengths and weaknesses are reveled when working as a team.

Volunteering is awesome and can have many perks however, it does come with a few stipulations and rules. These "boundaries" when you sign up to give your time to a greater cause can seem as down sides to serving; but it's all relative to why you are doing it in the first place. Volunteerism can be quite time consuming, involve hard labor (depending on the organization you are assisting) and does not have any financial rewards. It is merely your choice (unless made mandatory from some other source or institution) to place this in your schedule to do. This is why I'd strongly suggest that anyone planning to utilize this avenue as a stepping stone to socialize more, gain references, find what you'd like to do in your business, find your life's purpose, or just give your time to something beyond yourself to find an organization that serves an idea or community you believe in and have the skill set to improve and make better.

Moreover, volunteering just may be the vehicle that supports you in the search for your higher self. With that we seguay into chapter 8. In this chapter we learn some tools we can utilize in order to lay the groundwork for greatness. Within these next chapters we learn "how to" become Creatively Successful.

Chapter 8

Becoming Creatively Successful

So are you ready to be successful?
First start by asking yourself these questions:

- *What do I love to do?*

What is your heart's desire? Do you love to learn, teach, entertain, cook, travel, etc?

In your journals, write down a list of things you would like to do. Place the ones you are most passionate about at the top. Then, narrow them down according to the level of passion you have for each. If narrowing them down is too difficult, then take a hard look at those at the top of your list and see how each could fit into the other.

For example: If you are passionate about animals, are a vegetarian, and love to garden then think of how you will compile them together to make something of it. For instance: writing a vegetarian cookbook for cats/dogs comes to mind or creating a blog giving pet owners advice on how to start their pets on a vegetarian diet, etc. Think of ideas that are both creative and do-able.

- *What makes me so great?*

Think about where you are now. If you are working at a job you are not happy with, but you love what you do, think of what it is that makes you so great at this particular job. What capacity of it do you love the most? How can you get to the next level?

Self-actualization is important when trying to tap into talents. With this being said, the next question to ask yourself is:

- *What are my attributes?*

Conduct an analysis on what you know about yourself. Are you talkative? Do you always have a good hustle? Are you persistent, patient? Do you have lack of patience? Do you cook well? Are you a fashionista? Are you a great organizer? Do you like to be in charge? Are you compassionate? Are you always trying to give advice? Are you nurturing? Are you an extravert or introverted?

After your analysis is done, think of ways to be successful by simply being who you are.

Example: I love my career; but who I am as a person allows me to excel at it. I consider myself to have a great personality; this is what makes me so great in social settings and at marketing myself. I also have a great deal of patience and compassion for others; this is what makes me great in working with non-profit organizations and also in the healing arts. Lastly, I love to write, so in my leisure time, I journal my thoughts and ideas; this is how Creatively Successful was born!

- *Would I need to further my education in order to meet my career goals or can I excel without it?*

Colleges have a variety of trades, certificates, or degree programs to choose from. If your dream consists of something that mandates a certification, degree, license, etc. — then some form of schooling or training is a must! Please don't skate around this. You can get yourself into some serious liability issues if you get into a trade or sell a service by falsifying credentials. The cost of education and training can be expensive; but trust me, if you are following your passion, then the degree will pay for itself 10 times over, and the cost will be more than worth it!

If you are stuck between job and career, receiving a degree may move you out of this. In some companies, it may also help increase your pay scale. Going to college is a great decision to make for your future; however, I am not 'pushing' college on anyone. The final decision is totally left up to you. The purpose of this book is to assist you in finding your hidden abilities and talents to help you be content and successful, whether it be financially, in your career, life, education, and so on. As a teacher, I am definitely an advocate for education, but the reality is college isn't for everyone. You're your definition of success and the creator of your own path to it.

Respectfully, if you feel your talent is a money maker and college is not necessary, then make sure you are doing tons of research on your idea and have thought it out well enough to implement it properly.

- *Who do I know that could help me pursue my dream career? Am I a sociable person?*

Sometimes, it is all about who you know that makes a difference. Other times, you are the only person in the room you need to know. I am a huge proponent of leadership. My philosophy is to always lead and not follow; yet, no one can do anything alone. Some "self-made" entrepreneurs feel they don't need help in what they built by themselves; other's just have a hard time asking for it. Honestly, we all need that extra boost or hand from someone who came before us to help show us the way. Understand that it's important to be mentored before you mentor others. Leadership is having the ability to both learn and lead.

The Social Scene: Networking

Social gatherings are always good ways to network. Settings, such as fundraisers, nonprofit or community events, and parties are always the first thing we think about when you hear the word "networking," but have you ever thought that just sharing a random conversation with someone at the grocery store, train station or park could also be a great way to network?

In today's society, the cell phone is seemingly more important than surroundings. People also tend to go after influencers and people with high clout in the social arena, rather than mingle with or get to know someone who isn't well-known. Point is, you never know who you are talking to. That "nobody" you are standing next to may not be your favorite social media influencer, celebrity, or millionaire, but they could very well be the next. Make it your responsibility to get the most out of social events by actually talking to someone you don't know.

As an extrovert with an infectious personality talking to people comes easy to me. I do however understand how the flakiness and redundancy of the social scene can hinder you from wanting to network and bring out your introverted side. Believe me I totally get it. I've lived the life of an introvert for a moment because of the lack of proper communication we have with each other. Crowds literally made my eyes hurt because of the many energies in the room. I literally couldn't reason with my conscious how to connect with any one particular person. Not only this, but I couldn't understand why people were so competitive and sometimes judgmental toward each other. After a few months of being in hiding I realized that the introverted life was not for me and became short lived. I found that my power was in my words and actions and must be showcased within group settings. Understanding this allowed me to reclaim my authentic self and reestablish relationships with crowds.

Introverts and networking

If shyness is an issue, then the 'Almighty' Internet could be your escape. We all know about Facebook, Twitter, LinkedIn, Blogging, Instagram, Snapchat, and so on; use these to your advantage! Create an account and build business relationships via messaging and comments. Know that at some point, it's ok to come out of your comfort zone.

Overall, socializing — through the Internet or face-to-face — is a great way to market yourself and meet people that could help you on your way. However, networking can be rough if you are not aware of the right type of people to connect with. Understand that always being in the "clique" can be limiting. I am a living witness that if you stay out of the "circle," then you will prosper. Besides, rarely are circles loyal. Remember, circles go around, not up!

Marketing for the startup

So you have met all the correct contacts and you have some ideas on where you want to go. Now is the time to market yourself. What makes you stand out above the rest? These next tips are tidbits for the start-up entrepreneur. I felt the need to give this advice as a reminder of some of the things that may seem little but mostly forgotten when trying to get established.

Marketing can be tricky for entrepreneurs but your experiences will help you master the illusion. Here are a couple of tips on how to market your business:

1. **Know your target audience.**

Who is your business catering to? Your marketing ventures should be in areas where a large percent of your target audience is, so do your research.

Let's say you want to start an organization for underprivileged youth. First narrow this down. What exactly do you want to do with this vision? Do you want to promote education, teach life skills, find homes, provide meals/clothing, develop a community recreation center, etc? Find the best places to market that would assist you in your vision. Some places to market would be at schools or community events. Remember what I stated about volunteerism in Chapter 7? Getting involved with youth leagues, social services and shelters could help as well. Try to be present at as many events as possible, particularly those that suit your target audience. It wouldn't hurt to attend some that do not. (You never know whom you may meet!)

Branding

This is important. Your business should speak for itself more than you speak for it. The way you carry yourself professionally, your knowledge of the business, and your skills set (talent) should make you a walking brand.

People remember first and last impressions; everything in between is mostly forgotten. Think of a tag line or use your slogan in your approach to make a good first impression. Use the professionalism you want your business to exude. Your approach should not be too pushy or deceptive. People respond best to genuine business owners who explain how they can help, instead of those who rush them to purchase. In the end, always leave your audience with your business on their minds. Pose a lingering question or leave them with captivating literature about your business. You can even zero back to your tag line and slogan.

Use creativity in your promotional materials. *Here's a bit of advice on how to peek a person's interest.*

#1 Business cards: Your business cards should be professional and concise. They should NOT say too much nor should they say too little.

#2 Literature: The details on your signage and literature should be summed up in a couple of sentences, bullet points or paragraphs. People don't like to stand and read everything verbatim. People are also lured by flashy colors, visuals, and signage that pops — but this doesn't give you permission to go neon crazy. You don't want your materials to look cheap or tacky, but feel free to show your creative side.

#3 create a website: In the age of all things tech this may sound crazy to place in this book but there are still "entrepreneurs" who literally have not done this one task. We are in a time where everyone looks to the internet so having a website is extremely beneficial in promoting your business. A business owner selling any product or service should always have a website; and nowadays, a social media presence is a must!

#4 Cater to the visual person: As stated before, most people are visual, so create a display of some sort that people can observe. Be sure to place your tag line or slogan on your materials so they can remember you.

Example: There is an old saying that suggests people need to hear something at least three times before they remember it.

#5 Promote yourself fearlessly! Your promotional materials are there to be passed out, so why are they being tossed around in the trunk of your car or collecting dust in your home or office? Dish your cards out to all that will take them. This is what networking events are for.

#6 Know your worth! If you are starting a for-profit business, think of ways to promote yourself in a manner that is cost efficient to you, as well as the potential customer. Make sure to display what your business stands for through some sort of demo, speech or display. Unfortunately, most people feel that just because you are marketing your business, they are entitled to get something for free. A free demo is only necessary when working with a non-profit or volunteering your services. When marketing your business independently, it is your decision whether you want to charge or not.

This leads me to the next point.

Please do not short-change yourself just to get someone interested. It is better to first educate people on your product/idea, then work with them — within reason. However, be fair. Some people think they are worth $1 million (and who knows, your idea just might be), but come to terms with reality and come to a compromise.

Example: Health providers may pass out comp cards for a free initial consultation if you make an appointment with them. This way, the potential patient will get to visit the office and speak with the doctor first.

Don't be afraid to travel to different areas. Why stay stagnant in one area because it is where your office is located? If your business calls for it market to other cities that are near you. Some people travel for quality products and services. Don't miss out on a potential customer. **Be cognizant of the distance your willing to go, this is where your boundaries step in.*

Finally, keep yourself updated on current trends and happenings in the surrounding area. Go to seminars and classes that would enhance your knowledge and allow for you to be a better business owner. Environmental scanning is important. A smart entrepreneur will be one step ahead of their competition; i.e. themselves.

Contractual agreements

Short and sweet, you must at all times have a contract! A mutual and or verbal agreement is one thing, but a written agreement is totally another. No matter how close you think you are with a certain person or how nice they seem to be in the beginning, please, please, please read this closely. Get a contract! A single sheet of paper can change your whole business. Whether it is just the two of you agreeing to do a certain amount of things (MOA) or you just agreeing to do a job together — whichever way you go with it; get it signed by both parties. It is very wise for any business owner to also have legal backing. Retaining an attorney can be quite expensive but it is definitely worth it. Need I say again when doing business with anyone, always have a contract! That is all.

Chapter 9
Authenticity in leadership

Many people would be scared if they saw in the mirror not their face, but their character. I think we learned from Chapter 4 to never treat others as your scapegoat because you are trapped in your own fear. What you feel about yourself has nothing to do with anyone else, but everything to do with how you see your reflection.

Greatness isn't just for some. There is no need to be selfish with it; in various ways, shapes, and forms, it exists in us all. If there were a secret club for great people who all had similar gifts, then the sky would be overcrowded with crowns and capes. Celebrate your uniqueness, outside of the circle.

Truth is, people are watching you and how you "move." You are someone's mentor — whether you know it or not, so how you lead tells others more about you then you realize. Control freaks brandish their insecurities by trying to control others; people who are unaware of their power keep their full potential in a bottle just to please others; those who live in fear of failure try to control themselves by being perfectionists; so on and so forth. These attributes are no good in leadership.

A great, authentic leader knows their strengths and weaknesses, is very transparent with themselves, does not cop their style from others and utilizes their gifts to their advantage through delegation and being willing to learn from others.

Remember the days before reality TV? The times when you had to ask permission to use the one family computer (yes, the one with the big heavy back) and wait in line until all of your cousins finished so you can play space invaders on the Nintendo Atari until the cartridge ran hot?? Remember playing "Red Light, Green Light" until the streetlights went off? Remember when reruns of *M*A*S*H* lulled us to sleep (because after it went off, the national anthem came on and the TV automatically stopped all programming)? Remember when respect was a must?? Remember when not many wanted to keep up with the joneses (cause we all knew what they were all about)?

Now, it's different. Everybody wants to keep up with the latest reality stars, and teens/young adults are privy to basically whatever entitlement they feel they have. For kids, playing outside is either too dangerous or useless because all their favorite games are now on their smartphones and video games are basically virtual reality simulations.

It's unfortunate that this turn of the century has created a bunch of robots and not many people actually know who they really are. Too much time is spent trying to be someone else. It's definitely advisable to "get with the times" but also ask yourself, who were you before the world stepped in and told you who you were? Who are you now? It's not too late to remember nor is it too late to start on that path to figure it out. Let's lead by positive example and teach our youth who they can be. Things won't change until we decide to. Let's make outstanding discoveries to make amazing memories.

A follower waits for the chance, a leader takes it.

"Where no counsel is, the people fall: but in the multitude of counsellors there is safety." Proverbs 11:14 KJV

Chapter 10
Get Out Of Your Own Way (Stepping Out Of Fear and Into Faith)

Are you still feeling stifled from being your authentic self due to roadblocks? Comfort zones are generally created within the following three factors:

1. The lack of or continuous need for MONEY,
2. The loss of or continuous need for more TIME,
3. The preparation for the FUTURE.

Have you ever said to yourself, "I've always wanted to do xyz…," or come down with the infamous "IF ONLY " syndrome — "if I only had more money… more time… more love & support…" "If only I was/wasn't married… had/didn't have children… were educated… etc." These questions and worries plague us and keep us on the proverbial "couch" of life, which results in us never accomplishing our goals. Well, my Creatively Successful® trendsetters, the problem ISN'T MONEY, TIME, nor the FUTURE; the real culprit is FEAR. Remember we talked about this in Chapter 2? Yup here it is again. In that chapter I told you to place fear in a serious chokehold and prove it wrong through your actions, but now it's time to take a look at yourself.

Sometimes we just have to use the "IF ONLY" syndrome against itself, take a giant step out on faith knowing that you will always be supported. It is then and only then that you will be ready for the next phase/level on the journey and pursuit of your destiny.

"For God has not given us a spirit of fear, but of power and of love and of a sound mind." II Timothy 1:7 (NKJV)

To all the restless creatives, don't overwhelm yourself with thoughts unless you are putting forth action. Here are some tips to help you step aside of your own thoughts, fears and distractions.

- **Stop people pleasing.** You can't win them all, nor can you please them all.
- **Be open and willing to learn.** As we get older we seem to be stuck in our ways.
- **Stop trying to be perfect.** Progress is putting in effort, and you get an "A" for that. Be OK with being imperfect. We are imperfect beings, and that's OK. We don't need to know everything!
- **Don't ask God to guide your footsteps if you are not willing to move your feet.** The hardest break up ever is between your comfort zone and growth.
- **Be thankful for what you have.** Gratitude seems like a forgotten term to some. Humans tend to want more than we need, forgetting that life is the most precious gift of all.
- **Again, remember perfection is nonexistent.** If we had everything we wanted exactly how we wanted, where would we have room to utilize our God-given talent and creativity? Take time to look at the beauty in imperfection and not getting it right. The lessons learned might be the most beautiful thing in the world.
- **Clear out the clutter** of random things that are clouding your thoughts and judgement. Go and explore the beautiful things in life that sparks your natural creativity!
- **Go beyond what is limiting you!** Sometimes, you just need a brand new pair of "specs" — PRO-SPECT-IVES that is. See how beautiful things are when you go beyond your comfort zone!

Chapter 11
Standards of life & Business, Boundaries & Self-Love

Standards scare people. Truth offends people. Warning: if you really want to see who's on your team, have standards on how you'd like to be treated. Know your worth first and foremost.

Boundaries are your force field and your guidelines for setting the standards of not only leadership, but also who you'd like to be in business. Be ok with saying no sometimes and be firm with this. On the opposite side, be open to hear the other side out. Having boundaries does not mean you should be devoid of empathy; it means you are aware of your energy and the load you can handle from others.

Setting Boundaries

Nothing is healthier than setting limits for anyone or anything that will not enhance your emotional, spiritual, mental, or intellectual growth. Healthy boundaries are needed in order to keep the energy vampires at bay from trying to drain your newfound light! It is ok to physically or emotionally separate and move away from things that are not in alignment with who you'd like to become. Boundaries tell those who devalue your self-worth how to treat or speak to you. Your journey to self: (love) is more important than what is left behind. One thing that must be remembered is that we all are on various wave lengths and levels in our paths. If these people/things were meant to be with you on your journey, then they would eventually gravitate back to you; but never forget to always keep your boundaries.

Business Standards

The assumptions of other people can be a great distraction. Coinciding with other people's wishes all the time will only make you shrink, while the other person is proud of that accomplishment. It is best to remain yourself and not lose your essence. Be confident with your personality and new found gifts but be open to learning more about yourself and how to enhance them.

Please hear me when I say, you owe no one any full-detailed explanations about you and your personal life, outside of the product or service you are selling. Navigating through this is tough because some people feel the need to ask your personal questions. You are not obligated to answer anything if it is uncomfortable for you. Never think it is necessary to make yourself uncomfortable in order to run your business. Make this one of your standards /credos of doing business.

We already count the great, fortunate things as impactful, but remember that every unfortunate thing that is or has happened to you is too of significance! Know this, some people take, while others create. It is your choice who you'd want to become.

Self-care

All things are better on the other side of learning and taking care of yourself. Here are some tips for self-care.

- **Journaling-** Your life is a physical manifestation of the words that are in your head and the words you speak out of your mouth. We are all better people because of the things we overcome. Write down what you feel. Live with intentions. Your purpose doesn't have to be smack dab in your face. Set an intention to be or do a thing and understand that what you desire is coming full circle to you. Journaling helps you document your thoughts and those words that never got out to another person, or even to yourself. These words are a part of your emotional release, which can be torn up and thrown away or kept and reflected on months, even years, down the line. They can show you how much you've progressed on your journey.

- **Talk to a mental health professional** – Pride says, "Do it yourself." Wisdom says, "Find the right person who can help." You are not by yourself, and there is nothing wrong with seeking help. Talk therapy, as it's also called, helps individuals work through their problems. Seeking professional help from a counselor, psychologist or psychiatrist may be a huge help when it comes to pin pointing and receiving clarity for the way you perceive things. A mental health professional can be a positive means of support. It is quite natural to ask for and receive a hand when trying to figure things out in life, and it can very well be the means for your breakthrough.
- **Check on your physical health**– It is also important to keep up to date with your physical health. Knowing your health status is extremely important. Undiagnosed depression and anxiety can lead to other serious health issues. It is also important to get an adequate amount of sleep and making sure you are keeping a healthy food regimen.

Self-Love

Self-love is honesty. Know what you are good at and start your business based off that.

Self-love influences. It influences who you choose in relationships, the image you project at work, and how you react and respond to issues.

In today's society, it is almost popular to become some sort of entrepreneur. However, the fate of business is determined if it lasts 3+ years. With that said, many people ask me how I became successful in my business, and how I was able to do so many things based off just being in the healing arts. My answer is this: Had I not known myself first, I never would have dared to step into business. I opened myself up to:

- Be vulnerable and let go of expectations of others to heighten my expectations of God that is within me.
- Sacrifice and leaving everything I thought I knew behind to be open to learn the things I didn't know.
- Make mistakes, show emotion and forgive myself for what I allowed and utilize those lessons for improvement.
- Allow my craft to introduce me to more of myself.
- Seek counsel with my intuition first, rather than seeking validation.
- Be a sellout for my standards, self-worth and how I'd like to be treated.
- Take control over distractions and stay focused.
- Be as authentic as they come and never change or shrink to fit anyone's mold or opinions.
- Getting out of my own way!

I can't tell you enough how important self-love is in business. It goes back to the beginning of the book when we discussed breaking generational curses. Self-Love is something that a lot of people are forgetting about. It is the basis of our follow through in getting things done and understanding when it is time to rest. The footing and foundation of any business starts with having self-love and awareness within ourselves in order for us to function properly in our daily lives. In a world of influencers and platforms I believe every leader should lay this groundwork before they decide to begin anything in life. Knowing yourself is the beginning; how you utilize your full creative potential is the key to creating longevity.

How will you create your longevity?

Thank you for reading. You have successfully made it to the end of this book and for this I am grateful.

I wish you peace and self-love on your journeys

Tiana Allen, Author

About The Author

Tiana Allen is indeed a unique creative. She is a Healer, a Teacher, International Speaker & Entrepreneur that has founded several successful brands that all correlate to her gifts and talents.

With years of experience in a variety of subsets in business Tiana has a lot of wisdom to share with the masses. Success has not come easy for her. It was built off of following God, trusting her intuition and tapping into her creative sense. Tiana's foundations began in Chicago, Illinois but has had to make one of the most difficult decisions to leave her home town for the betterment of her company.

She is the Owner of @TheWellnessSanctuaryInc a healing studio in Atlanta GA where she treats people with chronic illness, survivors of cancer and domestic violence through Therapeutic modalities and Lymphedema Management.

She is also the Founder of The Journey Institute of Wellness, Inc. a nonprofit organization that caters to the underserved population by conducting yearly wellness events in the community.

Tiana has traveled around the country and internationally to give talks about Self Love and Entrepreneurship. She has also founded @SelfLoveRX an emergency kit that provides content for journaling, focus and self-reflection.

Last but not least Tiana is the founder of the @CreativelySuccessful® brand geared toward providing insight and advice to creatives seeking solace and direction on their journeys.

Please visit www.CreativelySuccessful.com to learn more!

www.ingramcontent.com/pod-product-compliance
Lightning Source LLC
Chambersburg PA
CBHW070957240526
45469CB00016B/1498